Fig

CAROLINE BERGVALL (b. 1962) is a poet and text-based artist based in London, England. Previous books include *Eclat* (1996) and *Goan Atom, 1 (Doll)* (2001). Her work has appeared in many magazines and anthologies internationally. A selection has appeared in the *Oxford Anthology of Modern British and Irish Poetry* (2001). She has developed audiotexts as well as collaborative performances with artists. Most recently, the installation *Little Sugar* for TEXT Festival (Bury, 2005) and *Say: "Parsley"* at the Liverpool Biennial (2004). A CD, *VIA: poems 1994–2004,* is published by Optic Nerve. Her critical work is concerned with plurilingual poetry and mixed media forms of writing. She was the Director of Performance Writing, Dartington College of Arts (1994–2000). She is currently Research Fellow at Dartington and co-chair of Writing, Milton Avery School of the Arts, Bard College (NY).

Fig

GOAN ATOM 2

CAROLINE BERGVALL

SALT

CAMBRIDGE

PUBLISHED BY SALT PUBLISHING
PO Box 937, Great Wilbraham, Cambridge PDO CB1 5JX United Kingdom
PO Box 202, Applecross, Western Australia 6153

© Caroline Bergvall, 2005

First published 2005

Printed and bound in the United Kingdom by Lightning Source

Typeset in Swift 9.5 / 13

ISBN 1 84471 092 0 paperback

SP

1 3 5 7 9 8 6 4 2

I admit not knowing very well what poetry is, but on the other hand quite well what is a fig

Francis Ponge

a fig fruit, a fruit of fig

Contents

11 16 Flowers

19 Flèsh

31 About Face

49 Say: "Parsley"

63 Via

73 In Situ

83 More Pets

91 Dog

99 Reading Ginsberg

105 Reading Arendt

111 8 Figs

131 Gong

16 Flowers

The occasion was an invitation from poet John Cayley to collaborate on his permutational text *Nothr's* for a CD-Rom by the journal *Performance Research* (Summer 1999). Text sections referring to flower motifs in Marcel Proust and Jean Genet's works were excerpted to form the basis of his "transliteral morphs" between the French quotes and their English translations. As a contrast to the additive and randomly changing structure of John's chosen weave of quotes, a white text on black background, I suggested that I would develop a series of 16 one-liners. Each line would be programmed to appear once only (or less) per reading session. One at a time, a black text on white background, they would interrupt for a few seconds the seamless flow of the structure.

The 16 lines were linked to the piece's quotes and translations through the italicised nodal word at the core of the chosen quote. They were connected to one another through a logic of agglutination, of concatenation. "Heart us invisibly thyme time". *80 Flowers.* Five words a line. A doubling of eight, amorosa entwines dolorosa, lines of words worn like crowns of flesh, vulnerability redemptive, the surprise of love is its most rigorous demand. "Certain acts *dazzle* us and light up blurred surfaces as if our eyes are keen enough to see them in a flash, for the beauty of a living thing can be grasped only fleetingly" *The Miracle of the Rose.*

1.   vagrant rOse *paths* compressed Come–on

2.   hover matin l'aRose in– *Mers*

3.   a–*glimp* th ornful umineu*se* darKorolla

4.   faint Fur st *special irrésistible*

5.   Lansoft –goRous elovelash *petals* absorbed

6.   small*red* Vibrant lovegash pétales embedded

7.   *White* throated flatfanned dressLash lovétale

8.   *PINk*draw –inGirls lovcrest pétalent Bedded

9.   looseHung metal Folds *Heat*–be ds

10.   heave–heavends Glissening *Hearts* be attitudes

11.   soar Coeurs formidable *foam* liS–p

12.   Offer inCuts alArm to her–*Throbbing*

13.   Offer bloodFalls hearthRobed inner *tHighs*

14.   OffHer *dazzle* bloodgush enrobe lovMeta

15.   lovblong *facegUsh* –er mettle ways

16.   un*Crowne* D–ashes dazed–in tHer PInCK

Flèsh

The occasion was an invitation to create an artist book for *Volumes of Vulnerability*, a millennium project curated by Susan Johanknecht and Katherine Meynell for Gefn Press (London, 2000). In the wake of the business generated by the millennial year celebrations, the editors were insistent that contributions should concentrate on "anti-monumentality". To this end, the budget was minimal and each piece would need to be limited to four A4 sheets (or similar). My work involved paying tribute to four writers who share a trance-like understanding of the connections between text and physicality, between violence and verbal illumination, between erotic and spiritual passion, and the intimate and public facets of a desire for writing.

Writing was organised through activities of folding and cutting. Folding four bright yellow A4 sheets, twice, lengthways, and stapling them together. Folding the title-page over the sheets. A gushing magenta. FLÈSH ACOEUR. To seal the booklet is a gluing of my name to the sides. A reader needs to cut through the name seal and along the folds for the different levels of text to open out. Each opens out according to the cut. These physical gestures would be lost to other formats. On preparing the piece for inclusion in Nicholas Johnson's anthology *FOIL* (Etruscan, 2000), the title was shortened and the commentaries were expanded on. Less bodywork, more language. FLÈSH. Another platform brought along its own demands. The internet version was developed with the help of artist Anya Lewin for the net journal *HOW2* (Autumn 2001) under the editorship of Ann Vickery. For this book, the compound "in-mouth, Vegina!" has been replaced by the head of the Regina.

Flèsh   according to St Teresa of Avila

Do you suppose a person in perfect possession of her senses feels but little dismay at her soul being drawn above her, while sometimes as we read even the body rises with it.

Things had been going Rather-Well. Sex-loot. Caravans of PushpUsh. Needy machines Easy To Please. Pissabout reFillable. Everything pruned happy as shaved. Rubbed A Fff in it long Enough to Suck-Off thereafter the stakes we'd lie in about. JUMPs the Surf with a Start. Off the ace. Now caught-In The Grip Of. Hot and tired. Row and row. Oars dig holes in Every Single Pie own I had ed absent-mindledly. Torn in the bell heat Kick-Up spare-heads. Something's knocking against the SKin. large persistent bulks In The Air. Brutally pulled innards. Gut seizure GONgs concave.

Flèsh

according to Unica Zürn

As millions of blood corpsules desert her as the countless red spots of an allergy cover her body she writes in her Manuscript of an Anaemic*: "someone walked inside me, crossing from one side to the other".

Red-folds a lot of bl. Bright deed. Dead trance. Who will Carry The Stuff spews out of the Cave In. Having the outline or surface Curved like the interior of a circle or sphere. What ddoesn't. Exhaust itself on Waste aWay on Contact. Engulfs the Surf's being Lifted Up To. The mouth of the rover. Banging under the skI. Explosion heats flans etc. Catches G Cold on Entering-rbit. On The Face Of It's nothing mined leads to The Most disturbing The Most proFound Apparitions. Always a Throne stow away from knowing which of the Tears profusely the Ho the Mo st.

Flèsh

according to Hannah Weiner

over the hill oh sometime myname
I was delivered from it

Reaching Inside a. Her bod Y retrieve Small lastiC ups. Meat is carved
all over th. Her insides. Bright were the. Daze. Pushing -error For The
Sake Of T. secretes incessantly. Pushing the boot if full corpse out of
the. my her. Tackle. A mouth-of V. draining Anatom Looking Around.
Actively Falling-For I was getting into bod. Y thinking this Giving space
might Temp for the corps du body for the body of my coeur. For the coeur
du core du corps body Another walkIn. Deep In The Hole. Such a Great!
Big irl of a Ho. Sleep wahwah walking. L-holds. Rare attentions to abandon.

Flèsh   according to Kathy Acker

I write in the dizziness that seizes that which is fed up with language and attempts to escape through it: the abyss named fiction.

Who held Girdles wooed held the contemplative To Hand that which I'd take for Genuflections I take to genuflecting. Takes me by the Keel-Over busts my Hopen Fans Out like a Muscle. Edible bivalve mollusc. EBb Reast lights the premises maddeningly live-matter feels no Hate no L. Go Figure s envisage a clea beach r coast m odes d'efacement. Entire circuits tRipping on friction. A face slow ed Right-Down revs the Grooves of Gyration comma the Stitching of Thought comma the Very Temporary Safety of Skin. AStride alights. L- Keeps. Hail. In-Mouth, Regina!

About Face

This piece was invited by the Liminal Institute festival, curated by Larry Lynch and Acts of Language (Berlin, Sept. 1999). An infected tooth had been extracted prior to leaving London. The sutured pain and phantom bone made it difficult to articulate the text to the audience. Speech fluency is an articulatory feat. It presupposes the smooth functioning of speaking's motor skills. It is a choreography of the physiological mouth into language. 45 minutes were needed to read a piece I now often perform in less than 15. This doesn't all have to do with teeth. 45 minutes is the A-side length of 90C audio tapes, a format which used to be common with portable players. Players were passed around to the audience with Heiko Fisher's unedited, spoken translation into German. They leaked another listening process into the real-time situation.

Such processes of marked physical and verbal impediments continued to be explored as part of the live readings. Traces of restrictive, non-fluent speaking patterns also made it into the written text. One is not a transcription of the other. Neither is the other a performance of the first. For a second showing, I invited Redell Olsen to converse with me on minidisc about the exploration of the face in visual arts contexts. This conversation was speeded up and circulated during the piece's second performance at Bard College on invitation from Joan Retallack (Nov 1999). To those who picked up the players, most of its semantic articulacy would have seemed erased, yet not the recognisable speech signals they provided. Micro-sections from this material were added to my live verbal performance. In time, micro-frictions from this live language were added to the written text. A marriage of French and English equestrian detail was taking hold just as my own conclusions were being drawn about the Mona Lisa as conceived by Duchamp.

Begin a f acing
at a poi nt of motion
How c lose is near to face a face
What makes a face how close too near
Tender nr pace m
just close enough makes faceless
too close makes underfaced

Ceci n'est pas une fesse
Settee nest past urn face
Sees inhere your passing

      This is not a face
a f s a face is like a rose
s easier l this
th n fss
correlated to ah yes tt t waltzing t change

When faced a point is found
        & many others
Everything you've faced not nt
fll pg not writ yet portrays time takn
writn port
Time taken stand in fr

When found a poin s broughtout
you erm n it poin t by poin
t racks the fat of lines
yet f
        aced markd distance

I'll always remember this painting because I couldn't see it.
It was displayed at waist height behind a chair covered with
glass but next to the window so that glass caught the glare.

Distance ac rossing needs ccidents
good fort
une a crossing that needs
            does beckon
quite li unlike
            each sticking pt
brings sepr
ate focus to th
is and to that

Dotted erm I thnk Ddoodling
            vry,
yes necary
            Sgot a strong eyebroil
at the end of
Vry, interst, -ed, mm

            At which p oint toface begins
a total part of what
cannot be backtracked
points rto impact at the enckline neckline
beyond the impl
gated c ated body limit

Face-corporeal signals a bulk
a corpsi congl, mm
            ration of means
-ng in relation to, what phase might be

            at arms length

Found as of
Shh at t time
the way it was procesd, was that a lasting relation to
Large face-markets exarcerbate the need
　　　Mm,
first a marker then a collection
　　　mm,
face-medallion fly on the coiffe
　　　mm,
Ccollect small figuresfigur eenes

　　　　This is not af
　　　　a face arise
A face arose is like
a redredlike a parting
likely to a pear is likely to disappear
mm, woo p ump, I was
facelike
Envisage brings on more

Likeday would, gn, you take yr
basiclly in yr han ds, whatdoyouf f
feel, actually takes notlike, w
Take my face in my hands, I feel warm d k

*More insidious more penetrating than likeness, the Photograph
sometimes makes appear what we never see in a real face (or in
a face reflected in a mirror): a genetic feature, the fragment of
oneself or of a relative which comes from some ancestors...the
photograph gives a little truth, on condition that it parcels out
the body. Unquote, page oneowethree*

Ss I mean, plotting
a face is pulled off from bark
-in language proudly

Ceci net pass une bride
a face not asa horse
yet horselike fits describd

This fac is a nat
                ural extension of the grid
Angled fact won't kerb, You can watch, zj, from afar
ok lick clock mends
Wa sj well there was no
Tsho see ther fete
Faces an objec ts
-ing, ov, ehm, Record immediate
                small technology,
speed up splinter shrapnl
                can hear the converse say
                Between the diff ehm erent diffrent
Timley clocks cheese-transcript
straight at t
doesn't even look amended
Camra face-tools
erm ed it small technology
speed up splinter shrapnel
fades on pap,
thass righ!
no, -ly speaking, washes out quickly in th l in the light

                This face is pulled off by
Ea t ing much fig
                uch eating choking on face
eating much fg ig chkng on fc
Veg erot, think about, -gnize, another would have it, th-,
mm

       figure prepares to faceload aF
acelike a redred rise
       this is not, why ox en, g, -ent,
ouldnt see, err, twiny, I mean not tiny

         Parting-like raised-like
like like like like
unlike unlike unlike unlike
     ly
       meet

A face encountered
            at first sight is not adored
tadored aface must exacerbates motifs of recognition
Saffaisse encountered is not
adored at first
sight yet
            syncopates provokes face
loadTurn abou tface

            Adored is a pulse
            Shudder face face adored adored
Shudder syncopate faceless faceless
yet when adored delight at this profound absenting
yet when unadored makes faceless
            Horror at the absented
Don wan don noeud
            another would have it here inaway f
            foreseeable at surface, n, the others are diff,
this is a, you know, layers
No pt of surf
                        Unlika doring
                        most unlike

Portray degrees of face acc to degrees of nearness
remove degrees of face acc to de grees of resistance
Whn faced a pt of nearness
            strikes a precarious balance of stillness
                        Then arousal

Its to beat at to nodonen
            vocab, pain sound
            only thi
stouch of red
to Rem ths b Fc by

Imean jool s bri if had that
        face-up for days
        loosens padding
        like amask dropsout
fall away a k caravan of faces, dust part
iclesMany ador
ed gather in one
fall to knead pain detached
likefaced from skull

        Show your face-bride
In yr !
Gr d grows a grid or plant-like
molec unravels
        type revered asound like
that Gone in one
        Unlike made likely
And the likeness of flies
Unlike made likely
Unlikely kept
unlikely

Taking turns with violence
a face is first removed then applied
react w/ face you think o
Taking turns with violence
a face is first removed and all faces standing in
Tezoo of efinitely but break as t it defacement pronounces
the triumph of mass
if think of ths non anon aggrave
excess of face made superstitious
soon a face replaces
another ssh ee Id forgot
punishing
word aff, f aux shoo, ehm, haunting, n face makes, in the, I
mean,
draw thng in
What hides things itself-like
What draws things out

and face will split
Face keeps
Who d enied kept faceless
Who denied burdened with face
Medusa had no face mirrored every face is a face lost
brought out the shock upfront

medusa had none who mirro evry face a los
S another narr nobody dzz theb edla urm widder repr
emptati then none
between the living and the ed

Face-wash
an need & the hum
Face-grip
Jus, -perience

Pig-face
      for that
Two-faced
      Our cult, no change
Fuck-face
      Its true
Face-stain
      In sight
straight-faced
      face-tap
face-stain
      like that
otherwise it's

Motion sparks nameless noise and the others are diff
walking up to taking turn
wid shame
      Look at the them!
the not
      non not
more-them
      more-non
more-not
      not-mostly
not-local
      less-local
than-local
      more-less
Then there's more tearing
      Then another Hanging
Good bless
smashed these f
ace sin
good drinking water from their skulls

This is not a fac is not a bride
and the-others are a diff

43

Admitted there was no
Face t remembered
        no rec
                a ffaced it will be for gotten
envisage a ffaced it will
have been forgotten
Moves and terrifies
like photographs, bones, bundles of clothes,
paint-like portraiture Francis
Bacon pulls at face and face enlarges
Now taking on loss hits on duration
taking on less for more
loosens padding
Bride-like composite
is the red red rump of the thin moustache
Like a curtain pulled a face it like a parting spectacle

        Functns wi
all senses shot out
        Facting evrythng
prtl dsfigurd with faces on
irons anythng out
with a sense that rubbing out
takes care of genetics

Face swipe rerun
Fac it rrun swipe stamp coin-face
A face it grid
A fface it with one eye
A ffac it anothr
A fac it eyeless
Purple blocks of matter
        likens

Y know said by
clokd the era machine
Lissening with the feet
iS a window
Not listening the, way of the
Ssually
Caught
In
Grooves
Sparsed by
Sets
Erefore facewipe
Double back
Face it rerun
Grid generic
And non generic aspect
Face up to speak
Re
Peat
a phase aphase
Y a some such profound dilemmas
and walk up to

ceci n'est pas une bride

Say: "Parsley"

The occasion was an invitation by Spacex Gallery in Exeter to develop a piece of work as part of their season *Patterns* (Nov. 2001). The season was built around the work of two Algerian artists, Samta Benyahia and Zineb Sedira, who work at links between Islamic and Western art. I decided to concentrate on speaking patterns. Slips of the tongue or of the culture. The space I was allocated was an old industrial building on the city's quay. Four large rooms on two floors. I invited Ciarán Maher to work with me. He's an Irish composer whose main interests are in tuning and psycho-acoustic perception. We spent much time discussing structural ideas, the spatialisation of sound for audience behaviour, organising materials, doing experiments and research. Increasingly, I found myself thinning out the writing, paring it down, reducing the materials, not writing much at all. Mostly, four white stickers. White "R" on a white wall. Yet being at writing all the time, by abstention, by a physical investment in other artistic or social gestures.

The background to the piece would be the biblical shibboleth. Speaking is a give-away. My tongue marks me out. It also trips me up, creates social stuttering, mishearing, ambiguities. Say what. The shibboleth provides an extreme case of speech as gatekeeper. The massacre of tens of thousands of Creole Haitians on the soil of the Dominican Republic during the dictatorship of Trujillo in 1937 is still perhaps the most recent documented example of such a shibboleth at work. For failing to roll the /r/ of "perejil" (parsley). This familiar, anodyne word makes the horror all the more disturbing. In the culturally pluralistic, yet divided, and markedly monolingual society of contemporary Britain, variations in accent and deviations from a broad English pronunciation still frequently entail degrees of harassment and verbal, sometimes physical, abuse, all according to ethnic and linguistic background. We asked people (Londoners as well as all kinds of regional and foreign speakers) heard in cafes and shops to speak a couple of words chosen for their tricksy difficulty yet familiar (i.e. English) association. Say, "rolling hills". The thick English "l" and liquid "r" are especially prone to pronunciation variations and were likely to emphasise the point. We recorded about 50 different voices. We also worked out pairings of words which were likely to yield the most variations on hearing. Pairs with dissimilar speech resonances: Proper/English, Nothing/Certain, Speak/Freely. The way the loudspeakers were placed, on two walls in the farthest room, each carrying only one word per channel, spoken an octave apart, was a classic psychoacoustic set-up. Listeners were caught up in their own ears, created their own sense out of what they

what they heard, moved around the room, piecing together the pairings only to discover more words in the recesses of their hearing, their memory ear. Some thought they heard Italian words, others Hungarian. Hidden or disused first languages resurfaced in this physical and social comprehension game. A grid of plumb-lines, pendular, pong-ping, punctuated the upper floor. Other textual occurrences guided the verbal transit through the space.

Three years later (Sept 2004), we were invited by the Liverpool Biennial to re-site the piece. The explicit progression towards a culture ruled by fear and xenophobia, which keeps its citizens in a semi-constant, semi-conscious state of alert, had accelerated since the first installation and the dreadful months of late 2001. Perhaps to signal this, we decided to site the piece in a large basement. Instead of plumb-lines, we worked with raw light bulbs, again attaching them at the end of long lines of hanging wire. We carefully hung the original voice recordings and pairings in various corners of the space. Everything seemed more ghostly, throwing shadows, floating in the oppressive air of the space. We also used a 2 minute edit loop from the video-document of the first piece, filmed and photographed by Gary Winters. This reinforced the palimpsest, pushed the line of sight deeper into the wall. Was there in this a desire for spatial-temporal flight? Can I use the projected light to walk through this screening wall, escape its endless looping of events? On one of the adjacent walls, in a metallic spray-paint, reflective in the relative obscurity of the site, the producer Josie Sutcliffe and I painstakingly wrote out a reference to a speech much picked up on by the media, made in 2002 by the Home Secretary, in which he advocated that bicultural and bilingual families in Britain ought to "SPEAK ENGLISH AT HOME".

SPEECH MIRRORS GHOSTS   AS IF
APPEASED BY THE EVIDENCE OF THIS
WHEN   I HOLD AT LEAST TWO
OR AS IF INTENSELY PREOCCUPIED
WHEN   I AM HELD TO ONE

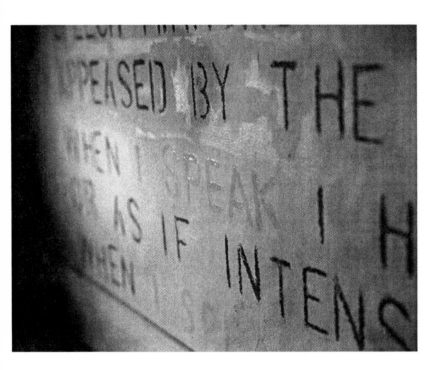

Say this language heels
language keals
over
S wallow in it
F hollow hollow fall low
S peak s low ly lie low
Say this feels c loose
the big mous th chokes
has a bong st r uck
in the throat
Spooks lulls angage anguage
Pulls teeth out
for the dogs
Keep watch r at s the gate
of the law
Say: "pig"
Say this
enflamed
gorge d
Say: "pig"
Say: "fig"
Say: "fag"
Say: "fog"
Say: "frog"
Say: "frig"
Say: "trig"
Say: "trim"
Say: "tram"
Say: "tramp"
Say: "trump"
Say: "trumpet"
Say: "crumpet"
Say: "crumple"
Say: "rumple"
Say: "rumble"
Say: "rubble"
Say: "bubble"
Say: "puddle"
Say: "cuddle"

Say: "curdle"
Say: "girdle"
Say: "gurgle"
Say: "turgle"
Say: "turtle"
Say: "myrtle"
Say: "mortal"
Say: "portal"
Say: "portly"
Say: "partly"
Say: "parsley"

Via

48 Dante Variations

I had started this piece by accident. Stumbling upon Dante's shadeless souls on my way to other books. Perhaps following a lead, in the dark of dark, in the woods of woods, in the sense of panic of the opening canto: 1-2-3 1-2-3 1-2-3 1-2-3 lines, and the three menace him. The panther the lion the wolf. The one at the crossroads. The one who needs. The one who terrifies. Then the one who calls, yet remains hidden. A poet or a hound. A perfect plot in the passing of time. Lost yet already walking.

Ever since the Rev. Cary's translation of 1805, translating Dante into English has become something of a cultural industry. Some 200 translations in less than two hundred years. Faced with this seemingly unstoppable activity, I decided to collate the opening lines of the *Inferno* translations as archived by the British Library up until May 2000. Exactly 700 years after the date fixed by Dante for the start of the Comedy's journey. By the time I closed the project, two new translations had reached the shelves. In all, 47 versions were gathered – once the two editions archived as missing, the one archived as under restoration and the multiple unaltered editions by the same translators had been disregarded. A fortuitous number that promised a musical structure to the list of entries and helped determine the alphabetical logic of the list's shifting cadences. In the summer 2000, a reading of the variations was made with Ciarán. Using calculations set up via his software, he unearthed an added line, an imperceptible grain, my voice's fractals, and we let it run, hardly audible, underneath the structure of the reading voice, inextricably tied to it, yet escaping it, releasing from it a surprising beauty, magnified shrapnel of interior sound. The 48th variation.
The sonic text was first presented at *tEXtO2* festival (Exeter, 2002) on invitation from Simon Persighetti.

During this entire process, some two years in all, it was as if the many systematic acts of counting and collating were carrying with them a motive interior as much as ulterior to the work being generated. The minutia of writing, of copying out, of shadowing the translators' voicing of the medieval text, favoured an eery intimacy as much as a welcome distance. My task was mostly and rather simply, or so it seemed at first, to copy each first tercet as it appeared in each published version of the *Inferno*. To copy it accurately. Surprisingly, more than once, I had to go back to the books to double-check and amend an entry, a publication date, a spelling. Checking each line, each variation, once, twice. Increasingly, the project was about keeping count and making sure. That what I was copying was what was there. Not to inadvertently change what had been printed. To reproduce each translative gesture. To add my voice to this chorus, to this recitation, only by way of this task. Making copy explicitly as an act of copy. Understanding translation in its erratic seriality. There are ways of acknowledging influence and models, by ingestion, by assimilation, by one's total absorption in the material. To come to an understanding of it by standing in it, by becoming it. Very gradually, this transforms a shoe into a foot, extends copyism into writing, and perhaps writing into being. This whole copying business was turning out to be a hands-down affair. This was an illuminating, if disturbing, development.

In the summer 2003, I copied out a 48th translation in English of Dante's tercet for a first printed version of the text. It appeared in CHAIN's "Transluccinacion" issue (Fall 2003) under the joint editorship of Juliana Spahr, Jena Osman and Thalia Field. This late addition broke the rule of the task, its chronological cut-off point. I subsequently removed it.

Nel mezzo del cammin di nostra vita
mi ritrovai per una selva oscura
che la diritta via era smarrita

The Divine Comedy - Pt. 1 Inferno - Canto I - (1-3)

1. Along the journey of our life half way
    I found myself again in a dark wood
    wherein the straight road no longer lay
        (Dale, 1996)
2. At the midpoint in the journey of our life
    I found myself astray in a dark wood
    For the straight path had vanished.
        (Creagh and Hollander, 1989)
3. HALF over the wayfaring of our life,
    Since missed the right way, through a night-dark wood
    Struggling, I found myself.
        (Musgrave, 1893)
4. Half way along the road we have to go,
    I found myself obscured in a great forest,
    Bewildered, and I knew I had lost the way.
        (Sisson, 1980)
5. Halfway along the journey of our life
    I woke in wonder in a sunless wood
    For I had wandered from the narrow way
        (Zappulla, 1998)
6. HALFWAY on our life's journey, in a wood,
    From the right path I found myself astray.
        (Heaney, 1993)
7. Halfway through our trek in life
    I found myself in this dark wood,
    miles away from the right road.
        (Ellis, 1994)
8. Half-way upon the journey of our life,
    I found myself within a gloomy wood,
    By reason that the path direct was lost.
        (Pollock, 1854)

9.   HALF-WAY upon the journey of our life
I roused to find myself within a forest
In darkness, for the straight way had been lost.
   (Johnson, 1915)

10.   In middle of the journey of our days
I found that I was in a darksome wood
the right road lost and vanished in the maze
   (Sibbald, 1884)

11.   In midway of the journey of our life
I found myself within a darkling wood,
Because the rightful pathway had been lost.
   (Rossetti, 1865)

12.   In our life's journey at its midway stage
I found myself within a wood obscure
Where the right path which guided me was lost
   (Johnston, 1867)

13.   In the middle of the journey
of our life
I came to myself
In a dark forest
The straightforward way
Misplaced.
   (Schwerner, 2000)

14.   In the middle of the journey of our life I came to
myself in a dark wood, for the straight road was lost
   (Durling, 1996)

15.   In the middle of the journey of our life I came to myself
within a dark wood where the straight road was lost.
   (Sinclair, 1939)

16.   In the middle of the journey of our life
I found myself astray in a dark wood
where the straight road had been lost sight of.
   (Heaney, 1993)

17.   IN the middle of the journey of our life, I found myself in a
dark wood; for the straight way was lost.
   (John A Carlyle, 1844)

18.   In the mid-journey of our mortal life,
I wandered far into a darksome wood,
Where the true road no longer might be seen.
   (Chaplin, 1913)

19. In the midtime of life I found myself
    Within a dusky wood; my way was lost.
        (Shaw, 1914)
20. In the midway of this our mortal life,
    I found me in a gloomy wood, astray,
    Gone from the path direct:
        (Cary, 1805)
21. Just halfway through this journey of our life
    I reawoke to find myself inside
    a dark wood, way off-course, the right road lost
        (Phillips, 1983)
22. Midway along the highroad of our days,
    I found myself within a shadowy wood,
    Where the straight path was lost in tangled ways.
        (Wheeler, 1911)
23. Midway along the journey of our life
    I woke to find myself in some dark woods,
    for I had wandered off from the straight path.
        (Musa, 1971)
24. Midway along the span of our life's road
    I woke to a dark wood unfathomable
    Where not a vestige of the right way shewed.
        (Foster, 1961)
25. Midway in our life's journey I went astray
    from the straight road & woke to find myself
    alone in a dark wood
        (Ciardi, 1996)
26. Midway in the journey of our life I found myself in a
    dark wood, for the straight road was lost.
        (Singleton, 1970)
27. MIDWAY life's journey I was made aware
    That I had strayed into a dark forest,
    And the right path appeared not anywhere.
        (Binyon, 1933)
28. Midway on our life's journey, I found myself
    In dark woods, the right road lost.
        (Pinsky, 1994)
29. Midway on the journey of our life I found myself within
    a darksome wood, for the right way was lost.
        (Sullivan, 1893)

30. Midway the path of life that men pursue
    I found me in a darkling wood astray,
    For the direct way had been lost to view
    (Anderson, 1921)

31. Midway this way of life we're bound upon,
    I woke to find myself in a dark wood,
    Where the right road was wholly lost and gone
    (Sayers, 1949)

32. MIDWAY upon the course of this our life
    I found myself within a gloom-dark wood,
    For I had wandered from the path direct.
    (Bodey, 1938)

33. MIDWAY upon the journey of my days
    I found myself within a wood so drear,
    That the direct path nowhere met my gaze.
    (Brooksbank, 1854)

34. MIDWAY upon the journey of our life,
    I found me in a forest dark and deep,
    For I the path direct had failed to keep.
    (Wilstach, 1888)

35. Midway upon the journey of our life,
    I found myself within a forest dark,
    For the right road was lost.
    (Vincent, 1904)

36. MIDWAY upon the journey of our life
    I found myself within a forest dark,
    For the straightforward pathway had been lost.
    (Longfellow, 1867)

37. Midway upon the journey of our life
    I found that I had strayed into a wood
    So dark the right road was completely lost.
    (MacKenzie, 1979)

38. MIDWAY upon the journey of our life
    I woke to find me astray in a dark wood,
    Confused by ways with the straight way at strife
    (Bickersteth, 1955)

39. Midway upon the pathway of life
    I found myself within a darksome wood
    wherein the proper road was lost to view.
    (Edwardes, 1915)

40. MIDWAY upon the road of our life I found myself within
    a dark wood, for the right way had been missed.
    (Norton, 1891)

41. On traveling one half of our life's way,
    I found myself in darkened forests when
    I lost the straight and narrow path to stray.
    (Arndt, 1994)

42. Upon the journey of my life midway,
    I found myself within a darkling wood,
    Where from the straight path I had gone astray
    (Minchin, 1885)

43. UPON the journey of our life half way,
    I found myself within a gloomy wood,
    For I had missed the oath and gone astray.
    (Pike, 1881)

44. Upon the journey of our life midway
    I came unto myself in a dark wood,
    For from the straight path I had gone astray.
    (Fletcher, 1931)

45. Upon the journey of our life midway,
    I found myself within a darksome wood,
    As from the right path I had gone astray.
    (Cayley, 1851)

46. When half-way through the journey of our life
    I found that I was in a gloomy wood,
    because the path which led aright was lost.
    (Langdon, 1918)

47. When I had journeyed half of our life's way,
    I found myself within a shadowed forest,
    for I had lost the path that does not stray.
    (Mandelbaum, 1980)

In Situ

It used to be easier to find genitals than to find a heart. Considerations
of what gives writing heart follows a period spent exploring the
methodologies provided for by its genitals. The personal (or so one
thought) discovery that art gives and removes genitals. The fugitive
histories of many of these anartomies. Looking through all things for
the markings and resonances that make genitals feminine. I was pressing
my hands down the keys. There goes an avid lover, a bad reader. There
goes a hungry reader, a lazy lover. For a while there was an immediate
calming order in the unfolding of erotic and pornographic narratives.
A few moulds to slip into, a few masks to adopt. I am the doll the bride

the merry. I give this up interchangeably. I give it up for a piece of S. In cycles of accumulation abandon disintegration. Easy and drowsy, aroused, walking around cages, drifting in the crowd, sweat covers this massive zoning place, this rising ship. Most of it adds up, which must fill her open subtractions. Like an hour-glass, each occurrence is tied to the previous one and leads on to the next through acts of possession and dispossession, possession and dispossession. In very tight structures, everything mutates wildly, constantly, and to surprising effect. Cumulative series make blissfully empty. Role-playing is more structural than narrative. Need disempowers. Need grows beautifully, it grows beautiful. Pleasure provides its own generative process of attribution.

This piece was invited by cris cheek for his *Language aLive* book series dedicated to "writing for live action or developed through live action or directly related to live action" (Sound & Language, 1996). Then republished by Iain Sinclair in his anthology *Conductors of Chaos* (Picador, 1996). It is the only one in the book which started out on the page and has had the page as its only working environment. It is ironic that it is this one which delayed, even endangered the finalisation of the book. For months, I was unable to set the piece. More often than not I expect that a project's success will, in the final instance, be predicated on how well or how thoroughly I've managed to break down, sweat out a succession of structural (and mental) shortcomings. It is emptiness which works the work, which tests it. How full is this structure. How empty can it go. How full can it stay. I removed the three column structure of the initial poem. I know now that a contented poetic structure is one that knows it is not a bed, or a megaphone, or an ironing board. I wasn't so clear about that in 1996. But I had rhythm.

[[

....,,
.............................w.........;;;....................,,,,,,,,,,,,,,,,,,,,.....

...e..........................t:lips.......over.................\"...................."........
.............""""""lll...,,,,
;;;;...................................tongue.............................7",,,'......................

:::: ....;;;;;;;;;;;;;press head;;;;;;——————*
into... ... ... _____ ;;;;;;;;;;ne............
.................................;,;....;....;...;.. ... .k:...................""""
[[

....: M,,,,,,,,,,,,,,,,,,,,,,,,,,,,,,,,........................:::::
.•..................................;;;;;;...::::::;;;;...
.... : ,...i.,,,,,,,,,,,,,,/////,,,,,,,,,,»»»»—
press................/..............chest.for.ch...............i.............................
..................'''g;;;;;;...;;;;;;;;;;;;..... ....;;;;
.............................`` ....´.EST........................;;;;
. ...;,,,,,,,,,,,,,,,,,,,,,.. .. ..:.. .·:....:..:.-:-:-:-:-:..;......... .....;
.... ;;;;; "p;;;; ....to......*;;;;//...............
 ''...mllo...... '''"'''"'"'"'"'"""chestto,,,,,,,,,,,!.......................,.
,,,,,,,,,,,,,,,,,,,,,,,——————·.__w___·..,,,,,,,,,,,,,,,ick...........;;;....
[[

> >>> > > >>> > ....:......................<
.:::::::::::::::.   ::::::::::::::::::..,,,,,,,,
.......,,.....//.............·....·.. ......:::::f:..................:::(........................:::i:..nd
::::,,:..slip.:::::.......;,,.....in.loose: >> >>> >>>>......fold..............
f;;;;;;;;;;;/;;;; ` ,,,,,,,,,,,,,;.;;;;;;;;;;,,,,,,,,,,,;,;l,j....oo.//////"'/......p.......
dare.move;;;;;;;..........................;;;;'''''''''', ,,,,,,,,,,,,,,""''.... ......
_____,,;;;;;;;;;
```
..................................................................:::::::::::::::::::::::,,,,,,,,,,
```
......;..moev.ader...//////..."'iUhy........///.............................·.............
......;;;..................;;;;(..........;;;;;.............""...................................:;
[[

--------......'......'.............'...._____ ....—·—
-///.........((,,,,,,,,,,,,,,,,,,,,,,,—————— tong:e ————————*———out.of.........

"" "" "" "" "" ""slide " " 2'.'.'.'.' ,,,,,,,,,,,sl.......:*..fu0p*.........
.....................,,,,,............./..,
.*. , ,,, ,,,, ,,,,, ,,,,,, ,, ,, ,,,, ...,.......
.................fan....................................... """"" ... ".. ", ,'"'"(((.................
,,,,,,,,,,,é.... .. ".......................... ¨ ;;;;;. ;;;;;;;))fan))))))))))))
::::: ::——*.... into ' ' ' ' ' teeth ' ' ....!.........*........•........
.........(tether.tether.tether)............2....::::. .. ..::.......::::::
.... >>> >>> >>> ....

[[
....•..............:::| |:.
::,,,,,,,,,,,,,,,,,,,,,,,
....;..
1....arm...............:::::::::oe........ve shoulder \\\\ ....//................
....over left//..../am '' '' '' ''' ,,,,,,,,,,,,,,,,,,,,,,,
'' ''......'' ''"'' '' '' ''...rub""""""""""""""""""))ø//......abd..................
belly.on.............." ..".....................gum.......................jaw......
:::::::::::"" :::::::::::::belly.on..................."""""......."""""""""".........................
.. ..2....................+...ome.......`!.N
;;;;;;;;;cross; ;;;;;;;;should;;';;;;;;;..................................."""""""...
[[
..............................; ; ; ; ; ; ; ;er.......................::::
..................w....pelvi.................////?kd.........fan..............:;;;.
...;;;;;;... .... :......:spu.....:::f.:...................liva..
.... f ....liva......
;____;;;____:::;;shsh:::,,,,,,,..22.12.94........./////.......................
.....bellion,,::::::::::::::::::::,,
,,..............."""""""""""""".
f1n;;;;;;G;;;;;;.;;;;;;.;;;;;;.;;;;;;.;;;;;;,,,,,,,,,,,,,,,,,,,,,,,,,::::::::::,
...........).)))).))))))))).))))-.)))))))..................))))))))(0117)9666125............................
throw/left...leg/over.((..(((((,,,,,,,
[[
,,,neck..................feel.sp1n.............................witH.....
1.eft.)....),,,),,,kneethumb..................alcu.........*..............brk...
....\\.|.\\\\.................................
......backspring.............................""";;;;rve;;;;;;;;;;;;;;;;;
_____._____............._____fan__.___.._____..
" " ' ' ' " " ' ' '.......throw right..................——-...............——
>>>>.>>>.>>>...legOver.(.).).).:......h:...heel.......""""""""""""""fan""""""" ....

77

tae..._toes....................   .::::::::::::::;;;;;....................st..........
...::::::::::: :::—acros:::::..arm,,,,,,,,,,,,,,,,,,,,,,,,,,,,,,,,,,,,.
‘,,,,,,,,,,,,,,,,,,,, ...   “”””””””””,,,,,,
[[
.....edge.off.high.rump.round.tong.insid.es.high....\/ v......
.\........... ...,,,,,,,,,,,,,,,,,,,,,,,,,,,,,,   “,”” ,,,,,,,,,, ,,,,, ,,,,, , ,,, ,,, ...
rsh...‘’’’’’’’’’’’’’/ABC/...... ///////////////////..................* • ....
...................((ighs ....//,,,,,,,,,,,,,,,,,,,,,,,,,,,::vlops,,,,,,,,,,,,,&,,,,,,A
’’’’’’’’’’’’’’’’’’’’’’’’’liI...........................th.....s.....................sp:::::
.....pull.breasts.inter;palm;:::::::::::::::::::::.;;;;...........int..........0
;;;f;;;:::.......................................oo........................’......
........................*......23.12.94...................:::::::::::::!........;........l.....................
.........ace!..........................””——kn • ee—_..............................;_-
......-.-slip’`````’`````’liversolar..........```imd..,,,...,,,,,,,,,,,
[[
—.——.wrap.breastsaround.hea.D..................................,,,,,,,,,,;...
........./*6....warped.count.outer.drip...::::::::::...;;;;;;..........;:::::
count.slapped’’’   ....
dr0p..................................(0117)96766125...........•:::::::........handEar......!
++: ; ; w:.....r..i..p..;:... arm,,,,,,,,,,,,,,,,7.......::::::::::::::*.......”
_____ é.............._____ —..—utterlapsein5ide lips................
.:.come.le.gs.ove.r.legs.suck.armpit5wit...........h....’’’’’’’’’’’
rasp;;;;;;;;;;;;;;;;;;;;;;;;;;;;;;;;pitswit;..............;;;;;;;;;;;;;;2;;;’
—————————:.com....legs.over.NeckPressoutbutt................
(((((((((((((()))))(96............)ba...)..)................................k....
[[
::::::::::::::::::::::::::>>>>>>>::::::::::::....................tearmuscle:.:::
on:split.ridge.uprawcrease`````````` ...````````````d
:pushouter:squee:zetonip:pleswith:.:......>>>.........fan...........i.../
.......•..................;;;;;;;;;;;;;,,,,,,,::::::::::rubFar...........................
.........................;;;;;;;;;;;;;.....................!..;;;;;;;;;;;;;;.....>.....P_(8....oP
...li*ht.................*swal6wswal6w*...........................
............3....2.............. fan..........519.............s1p...../...........,..
:-:::-!!-!!-:::........lifting.right.out.of.:::::”......’’’’’’’’’’’’’’’’’^¨’’’’
”................Mout*::::::::: ....
:::::::::::::::::::::::::.........(...............;kjh./;[l0wQ........././/..............
[[
.........................lo.....................wer,...............................

......................................:stretchthroa...............dnb..vc......
t.............,;,,,,,,,,,,,...;,,;;;;;;;;;;;;;;;;;;;;;;;;;;;;vfduy(*ifgh[;;;;;;..;
;...................nailedhai/.........**...........).....;;;;;;;,m;;''''.........er
..........................................................L............................
;;;;;;—............. stretching crack...........ued.....................................
<<<<<<<<......:.lim...............A.........<<<<<<<(0272)231570<< ?;;;;;;;;
<<<<..............//////////////////....................''''''''',''''''''''''''''q''''...
.... b. . ...onemJu....°∆.......................5..
..FALL.into.:.........................../:soun/——:...::::::ʃin......:e.........!!
[[
::::::::÷÷ sof÷÷......!...÷breav....E...
................................./.... Sp1ay :...............——................//..........
.... :.............'''''''''''''—————........ fan........................——
:::spleen::::::::::::::::::::::::::::>?....s::..........p...o//ole............- -...-
"''''''''''' • '''...........................
:.yhl,,,,,,,,,,,,carry ....Ma....................s.....................
:...s........o::..:.[;;;;;;;;;;;;;;;;;;;;;;;;;;.....................tly....,,,,,,,,,,,,,,,,,,
,,,........!` `~~ .... ~ ~~~ ~~~ ....////////*......./
: n crAck 6pen..............;;;;;;....... • .... • •......................................——
...............;.............lo...................` ~~ ....*an..
[[
.... • ....*an.............................. ....——
.ay!...:::..........................//
...28.12.94....................::::::::◊fifl°..................(0117)9666125..
•...•...........................•...........•.
:splaysplaysplaysplayspl*yspl...............''''''''''''''' :::..:..)))))
.lay.ply,.fans.ripple..wit..............///////..........................)gn.up
per.crack.bent;;;;;;;;;;;;;;;;;;;;;;;;;;;................ *an.....)))))))
mAB;;;;;...o=jdoaj.;l;;;;;;;;;;;;;;;;;;;;,;;;;;.;;.right,out..........
kk.................o.....scaled..nT......dorsal........./..............:'''.........
.........))))))))))))))))))(((((((((((((::::.*..................:;;;;;;;;;; • ;;;;;;;;;;.......
[[
.............................sc..................... *..........
handsigh;;;;;;;;;;;;;;;;;;;;;;;;;;*****............................. *an.........
eatair....................*an.......................line..........t
:falling;spilling;from;low;pores::::::::::::::::::::::: •..............::::
'''''' '''''' '''' ''' '''''.....................* 29.12.94....``````````.
:rav'n'roam''g 'ns'd e >y< e............................'''............''''''''''''''''

..................noise.....ound.................................//////...............
: .... ble'd'ng n'ck w'it' und'rl'p
((0272)231570...................................)))))))"""""""""""" ... """"""""""""" ...
+——ulp.........((0117)9662756)................................+˙.......................• •
[[
......................................˙...breathligament^{***}....//////Hlock.waist
(....'(l'(.........ai....eather.......................:.....!...long...ift...............
nt........oijoji.......................................:::::::........24.12.94..................................
:...say.ah.youre.fine.a.youre.fine.sucking.fannyto....::::::::::.
˙.......................˙("n...........................fanny.....................•.
...Runningcream::::::ply.ing.ton.gues.inpr.ofoun.did....-........
: : : : saying'ah'you're.fine.ah.you're.....................................
: :...............................(0272)231570::::::::::::::::::::::::.....................
:plyin'gongue'sinprofou'r'un'shin.splay.skin........jaw'"""
:devour.te'.....'droam'the...
[[
:::::::::::::::::::.˙an::::::   :::::::::::::::::;11..............................
:crush.wet.arse.with.full.harp...............:::...................::::,:,?
A****s • ..:.bUrn.delight.tinner.teeth.(.(...................,,,,,"******
..................**   ....12A.....................pril.....:::::
..!˙..............:::::::::.,,,,,hip... • flicking,throug,h.com8....again.....
:::::..:::::::::::::..:::::;......s jam.again.pore.by.pore.eating.jaw
................,,,,,,,,.............b*;;;.bit................*/..:::::::::::__˙..:• ....´´´'
—..—..-~~///~.....,——.ing.edge.ing.pour.fuck.from.lo..,P
................,,,,,,,,,.............................ni:p:::::::::::::::::::::::::::::::pLyE
:edging.laps...................edg.rimL0ops...............................:::::::::::..:::::
[[
:di/juice.full.of;jive.............................2..::::00.........::::::::::....5
....//;;;;;;;;;;;;;;;;;;;;;;;;;;;;;;;digging/juice/full/of...............
_____crackingthroatcr*ckingthroatcrackingthroat___[(....
:.spread.lipsover.cracked*spreadingVr*• bl..cracked............
..............................ho.tunder.gasp..................................::....h
..............................• ....**n..***....,,,...
:'.........burning.heap.slanting.arse:.lickingred.into.comb:
spilling.cream.into.space:bl.eeding.space.into.blood:::::::
...so.who's.so.what.so.Fanning.face.tow***...........rds.!...ah'y
ou're'ah.........you're.fine.run.ning.cream.out..........of.pur
[[

Rse.se.pulling.more.out.of.slant:pressed.soles.::::::::::::f...i
nding/br.eaksin.the..flesh:::so.me'times.chew.th'..to.........
ngs.until.gr***Ammar...toW....*[Hhowaaddistinctllackoof
ssetting[\Sometimes.actively..Reals::::::(and.turn.arou.....
nd....)i.*kssingme*.(and.turn.a.round:)whenCrackedpos.....
e.presents.its.self.to***s.peak:.....local.jargons.:excLam....p
ative.address(and:turn:around):......... ***.......and'...``.cusp'
!the.bones.that.5it.and.straight*.n.....::(turnaround)...r.....
emembering.sofens'the'view.:...sometimes.hard..ly......***.
remembered:5ometimes.what.clasps.me.thro•..ugh.th//
[[
sheat....[cwouldrrepeatbburdenaactivity[...........pulls.m.s
pat.out.syllabic:not:hyphen:ated:names:no:erect:.......Fa*
*mily.stone.(could.tell.(would.).*kissin***gyo*......exhibitsW
IPE.that's'loped.outto'shapeto.run.cu.es.....*issingm..*'''o....
ut.of.slippag***e((toanchor(...(toproduce((to(secure:(the~..
,.private.palm.is.a.publiCrack.split.........s.out.into.......arc
h:increa5e5.outofhand:..devours/them.its***.the.noise.in.
th'.mOUTth.of.SIT.deeply.conchlimb.deep.seatèd.d•e***...
...e.light.wells.this.hiG.place.in.the.world/this.hardfuck.i
n/your.view(swal***low)swallowco***me/again/.......w.hile.s
[[
till.barel***y.skeletal..pperceptionccultivatedtthroughuu
nexpectedffinds,,***swallowed.IN.time.wh,at.keeps.it.qui
et.is.the.noise.isn't'the.horror.absurd..tha***T........censors*
....out.the.food:.carry.,,,,see:HO..I.alway5.look.wHo.......al,
ways.loses.los***e.the.pAst.this.carrier:.........to.satisfy******"
.this.hun....ger:itscompre5ed.perspectives:the,,,,,,fla...N.
ttened.***dimensions:...of.our.macros:.........did.we.:.........
•.do.we:..come.out.hiding:.from.*f*.iction5:and:debris:.a.
nd.mucous:obs.essions:and...................se...........NY...
creting.forms:Gi***rls.insearch.of.noise.to.pony.....s...to!.*
[[
ponyms:::::*strut...rapped.inloud/.mu5c1econ5tructions.
.do..th.....j...;ok***05oh.:::::,,,.::archaeology.of...sax..and.*h
um.where.we.have.just***.***fans.........***Come...........from
.disperses.in.,the.growing.backgrounD..:.....aandsso.23.I.
ask.yo.nce.aGain:how.doyourememberwhat***youk.n8w.

More Pets

The occasion was an invitation by the arts journal *FIVE* to create a double-page spread for their re-launch issue (June 2002). A game of domino was developed using visual elements, small connecting signs. Hyphen bridges the space between two. Dash runs for it, marks out the place, the lines of a stretch. What if this connecting line is the very meat eyed-up by scavengers? Want to make one of three? Want to have disappearance? What Kafka knew. Spring 03 enforced new rules on all. Dividers box you in, keep you out as the dogs of the world ride the world to the dogs. This version appeared as "More Pets Less Girls" in Brian Kim Stefans' *Arras 5* online magazine (Summer 2003):

drawing a line at being a girl | being
like a girl | being like a girl being
a girl | act like a girl | acts as a girl
| wide as a girl |
| wide like a girl | widening a girl
into a girl | being as a girl to a girl
| as a girl from a girl | like a girl by
a girl | likes a girl for a girl | likes a
girl like a girl | as a girl likes a girl
as a horse |

I was out of town on the night of the reading and ended up reading these texts from Sangeetha's room in Cardiff. It was relayed live into the London bar. A distant voice coming in live from one receiver into a collective space brings a sense of urgency and of complicity. Vocal apparition, verbal rising. Always the shock of transpatial intimacy, of tele-connected physicality, lines are open, simultaneously here and there, now and then. As though the voice speaking has already died. And the message they're sending in is its transmission delay. The news reporter calling in live from. Yet not so much about death as about an intense culmination of aliveness. Your voice in my ears. The soundwaves of the voice are carried by radiowaves. What travels from point to point and gets picked up on the line. For all the seeming banality of phones, their increased mobility, the ambiguity of the contact made, unseen yet declared, continues to keep the time of a call, and the time shared during it, a mysterious and slightly phantasmic mental space.

Giles Perrings' simultaneous phone-in events, *The Exchange*, are live concerts in which poets and musicians call in at allocated times into the performance space and feed their chosen piece into his ongoing composition. I read one of Garcia Lorca's Granada poems, in broken Spanish, on a Summer evening, at 11.10PM from a noisy restaurant in Southern Spain, my mother doing the chorus, ¡Ay, amor / que se fue y no vino! // ¡Ay, amor / que se fue por el aire!. The tune of a trumpet-player calling in at the same time from St Louis just reached me.

On hanging up, there's a split sensation. Light-headedness, a slight disorientation. Spatial compression, spaciousness is sucked out of the closing line.

a more—cat
a more—dog dog
a more—horse
a more—rat
a more—canary
a more—snake
a more—hair
a more—rabbit
a more—turtle

a more—turtle cat
a more—turtle—more—cat dog
a more—dog—more—cat horse
a more—dog—less—horse—less—cat rat
a less—hair—less—horse—more—rat canary
a more—canary—less—turtle—more—rat snake
a more—canary—not—goldfish—less—snake—not—cat hair
a not—dog—more—hair—less—snake rabbit
a dog—not—more—hair—not—turtle turtle

a not—turtle—plus—rat catchat
a plus—dog—plus—rat—pas—chat dog
a more—hair—pas—chat—moins—chien horse
a more—chat—plus—horse—moins—chien—more—rabbit rat
a rat—not—plus—horse—more—hair—moins—canary canary
a rat—not—mon—canary—more—not—rabbit snake
a less—dair—mon—canary—pas—dair—dog—not—snake hair
a plus—rabbit—plus—dair—monte—lapin—not—snake rabbit
a plus—dair—rabbitnot—more—less—turtle turtle

a rabbitnot—catnot chatchat
a catnot—ni—more—ni—dogless dog
a ni—morecat—horsecheval—ni—dogless horse
a lessplus—notrat—monlapin—dogless—horsecheval not
a plusnot—notnot—notrat—goldfish—cancan canary
a notplus—snakenot—moinsplus—cancan snake
a snakenot—notair—lesscanned doghair
a nonnot—notair—plus—rab rabbit
a no—tair—plus—rab—more—turtle trtl

Dog

The occasion was an invitation to create a poster for the *LLAW* public-text series curated by Brigid McLeer. The piece was made on mass-produced xerox paper and was pasted up in Pitfield Street, London EC1 from 1 Nov. to 31 Dec. 2002. Readers of a piece of this kind are mostly and necessarily incidental. Commuters driving home, avoiding the Old Street roundabout, local kids living in the area, the fashionable art and club crowds descending in the evenings and at weekends into the Hoxton square area. Many wouldn't know about Kathy Acker and wouldn't care. The piece had to work so that this didn't matter. At any rate, calling names, calling out a name, making a public display of a name, meets all sorts of needs and resonances.

Reading Ginsberg

The occasion was a competition by Taxi Gallery (Cambridge, Sept. 03) for a series of postcards responding to the theme of "taxi". I was sitting on a bus, reading. In his drug-crazed, prayer-crazed, travel-crazed book, I came across a few lines. Sitting in the bakery window, I wrote down the circumstances for this find. Some time later, I gave the piece to Marit Münzberg to design. The colours of the book-cover would need to be the colours of the card. Deep-red lettering on an ochre background. Both dense and open. Both earthy and ecstatic. The piece wasn't accepted. By chance, a year later, I was invited to produce two cards for Text Festival in Manchester (March–Sept 2005). The curator, Tony Trehy, wanted a set of postcards by a range of writers to be distributed for free in the many bars and clubs and shops and galleries of the city.

reading Ginsberg reading Blake,
Indian Journals, 1970, page 146,
Bus 73 to Newington Green, London,
18.09.2003 at least once in the random combinations of happenings come
glimpses of recurrences, whether be dreaming of old friends
vanished by taxicabs, swept up into sky planes —
over London
or Maybe in Moscow — Such poetry as has seen the light —

Reading Arendt

This piece was initially developed for *Onsets* (Toronto, 2003), Nate Dorward's fund-raiser book project. It was subsequently presented as my second postcard in Manchester. Electric-blue, X-ray blue lettering on black background: the book-cover of my edition of *Men in dark times*. The philosopher who insists that personal lives are exemplary only at their public cross points with the broader cultural narratives that they entertain or find themselves taken up by. In her book of literary readings, it is the task of poetic work, this work of language, on language, to illustrate how individual writers have responded to the realities and responsibilities of this being-together, this communal living (for good, against its worst) at the root of what has been called humanity.

London, 2 May 2004. Reading Hannah Arendt reading Lessing, Luxemburg, Roncalli, Jaspers, Dinesen, Broch, Benjamin, Brecht, Gurian, Jarrell.

That even in the darkest of times we have the right to expect some illumination, and that such illumination may well come less from theories and concepts than from the uncertain, flickering, and often weak light that some men and women, in their lives and their works, will kindle under almost all circumstances and shed over the time span that was given them on earth. Eyes so used to darkness as ours will hardly be able to tell whether their light was the light of a candle or that of a blazing sun. But such objective evaluation seems to me a matter of secondary importance which can be safely left to posterity.

January 1968

8 Figs

This piece was initially presented as *Figs 1-2-3*, a performance collaboration commissioned for the *Sum of the Parts* Live Art Week at the South London Gallery (Sept. 2002). I hadn't presented performance work in London for a while and this was an opportunity to rejoin circuits I had previously been an active part of. Ever since my arrival in London in 1989, I had presented poetic work both in poetry environments and in the form of collaborations at festivals or in galleries, both in and out of town. For lack of the particular kind of time needed to explore performance work and collaborative forms, I had for the past year concentrated on working on my own and on the page. *Figs 1-2-3* was created in collaboration with composer Lewis Gibson and light artist Jo Joelson. From the start, it was a complex and doomed affair. Full of great ideas, unrealised structures, and fragile plots. On the night, it all just fell apart.

One of the sequences involved generating some writing live. Each word was to be spoken, spelt out, while writing one letter on top of the other until the reading of it is obscured.
A-T-T-H-E-E-N-D-O-F-T-H-E-DA-Y-I-T-G-E-T-S-D-A-R-K.
As I started writing, the mic tied to the marker-pen crashed with a loud

bang. Contact mics underneath the pad didn't respond either. By pressing harder on the thick drawing pad, the sound of the pen on the page produced just enough writing-noise to be heard in the vast, boomy gallery space. Mics had been adjusted to emphasise some of the frequencies of the voice and reduce the resonant, muddy space. The mics on my voice went dead. I had to place extra weight on my pronunciation, speak extra slowly and clearly, to be heard at all. A film of black ampersands on white background, which had worked pretty well for the first ten minutes, suddenly crashed and the blue light of the data projector illuminated the space. For 40 excruciating minutes, each section of the work bowed out. When all the technology was gone, what was left was my reading voice, the written display of the three main texts and the audience in the space. No performance bookings ever came out of this event and contacts and friendships within the circuit evaporated. Yet there was something extraordinary about this stripping away and the very public manner in which it had happened.

After about half a year, the writing resumed. *8 figs* was published as an *Equipage* chapbook by Rod Mengham (Cambridge, 2004). 8 texts and 16 ampersands across 48 sides. Marit Münzberg worked with me on the textual design. In New York, the visual artist Morgan O'Hara selected 1 ampersand for her curated exhibition *Drawings for Peace*, Kentler International Drawing Space (Brooklyn, Dec 2002). The film of 64 ampersands was reworked, reversed (white ampersands on black background) and presented at *TextFestival* (Manchester, 2005). A speck of light at the other end of the room. It's only when you draw near that you can see, it's constantly changing, at a regular, pulsating beat, one white & at the heart of a plasma screen.

Fig 1 is a pattern.
Better envisaged for what it is
than for what it isn't.
Like most things mostly envisaged
for what it isn't
nor for what it does
which is difficult to grasp
as a whole mostly gauged in its detail.
Purpose hardly
pursued, yet overdetermined.
A purple fig is purple first.
A detail whole in time.
Testimony sought
not felt will be and so it is
unrecognisable
according to pain, bread and gain.
Shadowplay is a matter of gradation.
Likeness is constrained and image trauma
wants nothing of language
but rhetorics and stigmas.
A quality in the light of performance makes active
yet out of action, until possessed.
Objects have the advantage of keeping still
or so it seems, holding the door up
until it disappears.
Ornate brass work and gold leafs
honour the joins and the passing.
Dissipating a shape accordingly
or better still, with volume to share.
To seem more seen when gone.
A hand-out deals with chalk marks and leather pieces.
Here in the sense of making.

&

Fig 2 is a pattern.
As such a gradual development
like a fruit, or a face.
Purple is purple, grows more purple
more-purple then less, more-blue than red,
more blue then black, then more-black than blue.
Colour breaks out.
Leaves comatose ring around the mouth spreads like a memory
one hasn't formally had, yet intensely familiar.
Neither returning nor gone
not approximated in language nor in promises of language.
Like one talks of the promise of an age
or the promise in a name in a gender in a field
or the promise in a figure.
Hidden losses for pride of achievement.
Comes out in blotches, excitations, phantom limbs.
Intimacy has no private matter or too much of it
that carries no propriety in the ways of the world
nor family status.
Green belly shitting red.
Yet a lineage that exists in the insistence of form.
Observing a form as one observes tranquillity
or a period of silence
or an invitation.
To act so that today will matter in form.
Fruit-time and ligatures.
Piles of blue candies and translucent
strings of beads.
Trajectory followed from radiant thought to solid contours.
Making sense of less, or with less.
Hardly in the sense of doing
yet a time for staying.

&

Fig 3 is a pattern.
Delicate and poised to grasp
equilibrium from one
side to the next.
Not all sides as one nor at once.
Cubic light consists of
one-side pr. head.
Eager to reconcile
by not cutting away.
Separate and divided.
Disperse a fig into a fruit.
Intricate finely chiselled
held up to public domain.
Beauty specific
in light of status and use
in light of customs of kinship.
Observing intermittent
periods of disengagement.
Favoured is articulate and cautious.
Gathering traces of activity
such as peelings, scrappings
of speeches, clippings into
dust-piles with a hard broom.
Macerating in plants.
Not too hot, not too cold
not too fast, not too much.
Nothing dying to come out.
Preparing for light in the night.
Keeping wet before wed
or wet not wedded.
Better still, wet embedded.
Things will move accordingly.

&

Fig 4 is a pattern.
A verification of means and of measure
as in safeguard.
Fear works against.
What gets applied follows recognition.
Being recognised as a part to play.
Misrecognised generates the most dedication.
A second glance requires more time.
In this way, there is much movement
yet little motion and many ways
to let rip are laid out not seen.
Language takes on where memory won't stick.
Simplifying to remember not
to deny
a feel for fruit
a touch of fruit.
No-place called home
nor home from home.
Yet not as divided as might first be assumed.
Invested proximity
makes clear a new citizenry.
Temporary subject to broken rule.
Homegrown buried shame with invitation.
Nor as separate.
Assemble to disperse.
Ghosting a range of activities
such as writing, eating, fucking.
For a while, I feel nothing I think nothing.
Held securely is not a bad position to be in.
Has many holdings
some to store.
Things will move accordingly.

&

Fig 5 is a pattern.
Tried and tested, reassuringly simple.
Reciting for template
much later for accuracy.
Copying, mimicking up to a point
of address.
Speaking in turn, artfulness cultivates
avoidance, yet care nourishes when weakened.
Disbelief is a matter of gradation.
Much of it in the yellow.
Enough brightly blinds.
What truth speaks for me, ghosts me.
Protracted hold-ups, a build-up of contraptions.
Shock demands testimony
magnified shrapnel
of internalised sound, to reconcile.
Taking counsel in detail bears fruit.
Accordingly I follow.
Finding nourishment in catching up.
To start counting as one keeps count.
Not to expect, nor to conjure up
not the right one just to sing.
Seeking guidance is a release
applies method to heart.
Breaking the skin of that spell.
Breaking down as small as can get
counting sticks and modelling figs
shaping thought in action
and the first
time of the first day
by the river.
Bliss for the smell of Spring grass.

&

Fig 6 is a pattern.
Unclear at first will be clarified.
Clarity released by resolve.
This vastness is humbling.
At first fearful, I adjust my every move
to the sound of known voices
spell out names
called, given, taken.
Stick to the skin, generate cold sweat
repeatedly undermine
determination.
Pressing on, the air
gathers around skin is a double impression.
Raising the stakes of sobriety.
Scenes open out beyond family romance
claim for me other ghostings.
"Is there not anything in you
dying to come out".
This dilemma for years.
Entangled spheres of activity
and non-activity.
The scrupulousness of poetry.
Thinking that functions in shields and openings.
Catching one's breath and holding one's breath.
Walking around with a notebook full of quotes
concerned with Speaking that is tangible and effective.
A kind of fighter who doesn't fight by definition
and aligns herself to the temper of friendship.
Pouring new wine into new glass.
It is ridiculous
both civic and miraculous
to be writing.

Fig 7 is a pattern.
Outlined is easy to make out.
Yet what could be blue seems green.
What could be slanted seems straight.
Spending the day in the company of guests.
In the absence of friends
we exchange casual words
about the state of law
and share our wine in large glasses
at this banquet of sorts.
Distrusting of language
each we begin to disregard
that all we know of one another
nothing but headlines, habits and phobias
not intellectual disposition, nor the way each we handle
personal transactions given the public mood.
A quality of apprehension
in light of the times.
Yet public challenge now possible article 14
"on any ground such as sex, race, colour
language, religion, political or other
opinion, national or social
origin, association with a national
minority, property, birth or other status".
Some move accordingly into the kiss.
Sentries stand still.
Force accumulates
archaic violence.
Kissing for keeps doesn't change much on balance
yet acting out fruit-shaped
brings a time for replies
and for replying.

&

Fig 8 is a pattern.
Loud and brash.
Uneven and exacting.
Carries colour from colour
into the open skull
shifts bones about, illuminates the heart.
She settles in as she starts to speak.
Courage moves red into the blue.
The call is patient
having sat long enough to stand by it.
Acts of poetry
as offshoots of writing.
Engaged when calm
engaged when in-shape.
What is being proposed.
Any count exceeds its own measure.
Cleaning up my
Act so that today matters for love.
Declaring conviction beyond the first count
of the first brazen song
queries the demarcations
of intimacy.
Any trace of certainty
conceals a panoply of methods.
The conditions of love that condition poetry.
What is inherited
of what is found
needs testament, not archaeology.
Here in the sense of being.
To have my fig
be a fig in the world
and all that moves accordingly.

&

Gong

The occasion was a call for "performance recipes" ("250 ways to prepare performance art") sent round by La Centrale Galerie Powerhouse in Montreal in the Spring 02, to be selected and executed by female practitioners based in Montreal. These are the notes I sent along with the performance structure. In response to your brief, I'm interested in setting up connections between external and internal transport. In the literal sense of public transport and in the sense of inner space, inner transport: how the experience of personal time in social networks inflects the approach to making work. I want to see how I can use traces or clues of such activity (non-activity) as performance instructions. I'm particularly interested in the fact of doing very private and invisible work in London where I live, to facilitate a potentially more public piece in Montreal. The way both aspects could become coextensive. I've decided to use the central section (zone 1) of the London Underground. I've listed stations in alphabetical order and have ended up with 19 stations. It takes 18 journeys to go from station to station. I've mapped out the interchanges. This pattern between discontinuity and continuity is an inner pulse or structuring rhythm. I travelled for 3 consecutive days, making 6 journeys per day, collating the time needed to reach each point. The pressurised air, the frequent delays and the brusque motions of the trains become increasingly demanding. In this confined and oppressive space, it is necessary to find ways of feeling safe and of passing time. From late evening on, it is difficult to feel safe. London, 9 10 11 July 2002.

I added a diagram. The organisers published this gently obtuse piece along with its main instruction: play for time. Going back to the piece a year later, I decided to retain some of the constraints of the previous year. I would set aside 3 days to get to grips with this structure. I wanted to understand the mode of activity which had been the most prominent and disorientating feature of the previous year's method: inactivity, or more precisely, in-action. The in-action of sitting on a tube, being carried by public transport, following a private map of instructions, held for hours in this situation, it makes no sense at all but through the fastidiousness and peculiar kind of dedication necessary to see the task through. Certainly, a mole-like approach to being at writing. It struck me that, if anything, this was quite close to meditation. For the next 3 days, I decided to clock the time and used these times to structure 3 drawings, 3 sets of lines, one per day. Detail brings about dedication. On the day after the project's third and final day, drawing lines turned to writing lines.

A first version of this project was published by Rachel Levitsky and Erica Kaufman for their vital feminist imprint Belladonna and launched at a reading for it in New York (Feb. 04). Drawn lines drew time and won't be touched. Written lines could be reproduced and were restructured. The title is from an overheard snippet of conversation between two boys, sitting across me in a tube carriage:

-   how do you spell that?

-   g - o - n - g.

7 july 2003 – 30 lines

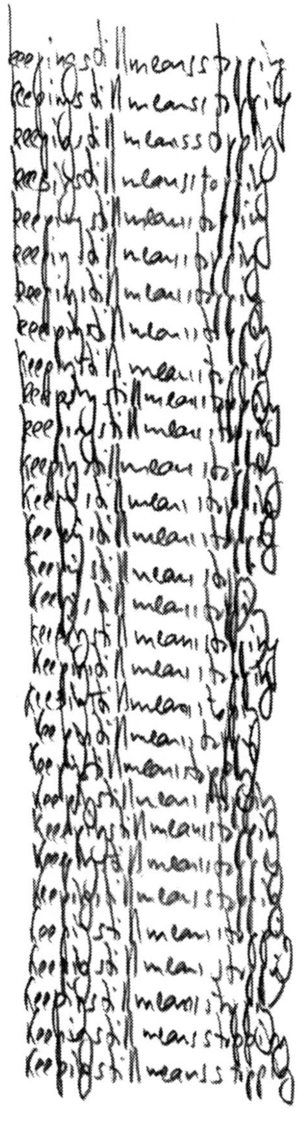
keeping still means stopping

8 July 2003 – 21 lines

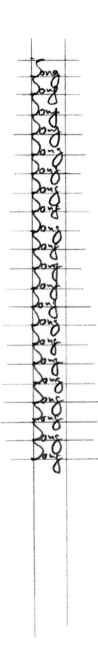

10 July 2003 – 3 lines

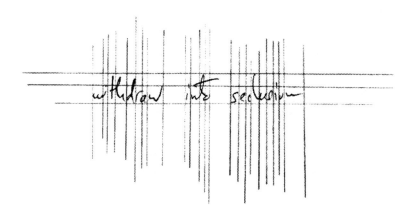

139

11 july 2003 – 48 lines

My mother is playful, has a generous spirit, who teaches integrity.
My father is steadfast, remains alert, who seeks inner calm.
The woman with the white hair shows me how to whistle
       two fingers pushed against the tongue.
The boy on the island has a salty mouth.
Alicia wants to pull me up into her bed.
My grandmother reads Teilhard de Chardin, boils broccoli on Sundays.
Dominique explores without restriction, flesh takes hold in my body
       turns as it turns to love.
The boy in the back of the car with his hand on my breast.
Guri is my first collaborator who's precise and works without gloss.
My grandmother smells of rose perfume, lives 33 rue de Vaugirard.
Derek Jarman tends an open garden on his illness.
Monique Wittig writes fiercely
       this great need in the love of women
       this great violence towards the love in women.
My teacher doesn't intercept the course of sex, lets the children play.
Cathy de Monchaux' sculptures are doorjoins
       rows of chalked up leather-pouches
          crushed lips, whitened scarabs.
My doctor applies ointments, heals physical and emotional shame.
The boy on the carpet with the smooth chest and his cock in the evening air.
The voluptuous girl in the room at the far end of the corridor
       has had us all.
Cherry wears a tartan at the opening.
Rod is soft and amused.
Rachel Whiteread casts resins in negative space, shimmer in the gallery.
My sister has fire in the heart, understands fear and takes her chances.
Jo is constant in friendship, shares in salacious tales and trains her body.
Stacy writes the grammar of birds, the suddenness of diving.

The dry sound of snow.
Morton Feldman in the Rothko Chapel.
Sally's hair is red and full.
The boy in the square is gentle and playful,
       the grass is moist under the moon.
Krzysztof Wodiczko provokes dialogue through
       high-tech Mouthpieces, Alien Staffs.
Romana is thoughtful, works from doubt as much as conviction.
My brother is opinionated and good-humoured, keeps his door open.
cris is joyous about art, eats with friends, collects all kinds of pieces.
The girl laughing ejaculates in my hand.
Felix Gonzales-Torres leaves the fewest of traces.
The beautiful girl spreads over me in the American hotel, I'm drinking
       too much, I'm generating a lot of fear.
Amin Maalouf reads the Rubaiyyat from Paris.
Lorca enters the song.
Cixous climbs the ladder of her name.
The black virgin is in everything.
My healer encourages meditation, demands responsibility.
My aunt keeps the bhagavid-gita in her car-door.
Harriet speaks her mind, holds her head up.
The first global march, 15 Feb. 2003.
My admiration for Arundhati Roy's positioning as a public intellectual.
Edmond Jabès writes that a writer is accountable
       also for what they choose not to write, for silence kept.
Hiroshi Sugimoto photographs seascapes, cinema screens, architecture
       radiant light in time
              "just air and water".
Josie holds emotional depths, builds on love
       who teaches forgiveness.
My niece's feet are soft and clear.
Hamish Fulton's no walk no work.

Thank You

Anya Lewin. Brian Kim Stefans. Catherine Ganot. Charles Bernstein. Chris Hamilton Emery. Ciarán Maher. cris cheek. The Electronic Poetry Review. Gary Winters. Harriet Evans. Ian Davidson. James Burstall. Joan Retallack. Joey Attawia. Josie Sutcliffe. Karen MacCormack. Kenny Goldsmith. Leslie Scalapino. Lois Keidan & Daniel Brine (LADA). Marit Münzberg. Marjorie Perloff. Nicky Marsh. Nthposition. Queen Street Journal. Rod Mengham. Romana Huk. Simon Persighetti. Tom Trevor (Spacex Gallery). Tony Trehy.

Printed in the United States
135055LV00002B/3/A

9 781844 710928